What's Your Name?

And Other Poems

written by

Hilary Weisman

**with illustrations by
David H. Huckins
and Sheila Foley**

Discovery Enterprises, Ltd.
1995

Discovery Enterprises, Ltd.
ISBN 1-878668-42-0
Library of Congress Catalog Card Number 94-71901

Printed in the USA
10 9 8 7 6 5 4 3 2 1

Subject Reference Guide

Weisman, Hilary
What's Your Name and Other Poems
with illustrations by
David H. Huckins and Sheila Foley

1. Juvenile Poetry
2. Juvenile Literature

Table of Contents

When I'm an Adult

When I'm an adult
I'll be exactly the same as I am now,
only taller, I guess.
But I won't make **my** kids eat stringbeans
or go to bed early.
I'll let **my** kids have a pet monkey if they want to,
and they can keep their rooms as messy as they want.
In fact,
I'll let **my** kids make **all** the rules.
They can make the shopping list
and buy things only from
the junk-food group,
if they want to.
They can get a dog
and a cat too, if they want to.
They can get one hundred cats ,
because they'll make **all** the rules.
They can make **me** feed the dog
and the monkey
and the cats.
And, they can make **me** go to bed early.
Hey...wait a minute...

What's Your Name?

I once had a friend named
motorcycle-lips-
purple-smoke-
upside-down-
sreaming-jazzy-pudding-feet-Charlie.
Or at least that's what they called him.
Everyone, except for his teacher.
His teacher was sure that
his name was just plain old Charlie.
"Just plain old Charlie," she would say,
"Can you tell us the answer to 2 + 2?"
Well...
motorcycle-lips-
purple-smoke-
upside-down-
screaming-jazzy-pudding-feet-Charlie
didn't like to be called just plain old Charlie
and his motorcycle lips
would rev-up like a truck on the highway,
and purple smoke would blow from his ears,
and he would do a headstand on the desk,
with a sound coming from his mouth
that was ten times as crazy as opera music,
and those silly pudding feet would do a dance
in the air, like a bug overturned,

and the teacher would stand in the front of the class
tap, tap, tapping her yardstick
which reached all the way
from the front of the room
to the second desk in the third row, which was
motorcycle-lips-
purple-smoke-
upside-down-
screaming-jazzy-pudding-feet-Charlie's desk,
and like this they did stay,
the teacher tap, tap, tapping the minutes away.
Until finally,
motorcycle-lips-
purple-smoke-
upside-down-
screaming-jazzy-pudding-feet-Charlie-
settled back into his seat,
and his motorcycle lips sounded
more like the purr of a cat,
and his pudding feet
gently kicked the bottom of his desk,

and the shreiking noise became ten times
less crazy than opera music,
and the purple smoke was as harmless as a cloud,
and he said,
 "Teacher, I respect you very much.
I do not call you 'Old Brown Dress Teacher.'
I do not call you 'Grumbly, Mumbly Teacher.'
I do not even call you
'Teacher de la Fingers of Yellow Chalk.'
My real name is
motorcycle-lips-
purple-smoke-
upside-down-
screaming-jazzy-pudding-feet-Charlie.
Nothing more...
Nothing less.
And that is what I like to be called.
It's as simple as 2 + 2 = 4."
And with that, the teacher came forward
and placed a gold star on
motorcycle-lips-
purple-smoke-
upside-down-
screaming-jazzy-pudding-feet-Charlie's
forehead, because he knew his math.
And then she wrote
motorcycle-lips-
purple-smoke-
upside-down-
screaming-jazzy-pudding-feet-Charlie
on the blackboard,
just to make sure she had it right.

The Swimmer

Allison Wiggums went swimming one day.
She swam in the lake and she wanted to stay
when her mother called "Dinner time, Allie, come home!"
She put her hands on her hips and she let out a groan.
"I'm swimming," she said, *"and I'm not quite yet done.*
So dinner can wait while I'm having some fun."
Then she took off her towel and jumped back in the water.
She swam twice around, that stubborn young daughter.

A few minutes later, her mother did scold,
"The sun's going down and your food's getting cold."
"I'm not hungry," said Allison, *"dinner can wait.*
At night when it's dark out the swimming is great."
So Allison swam, she swam all the night long.
She swam in the moonlight, she swam straight,
    she swam strong,
Then she heard the birds chirping, just before dawn.
She was swimming the crawl
    when she started to yawn.
And then from back home she heard her mom call,
"Allison, come home now. Once and for all!"

So Allison stopped swimming
    and went back to her house.
She crept in the back door as quiet as a mouse.
"ALLISON!" shrieked her mother,
    "You're wrinkly and wet,
if you keep up this swimming, you'll get me upset."

"I'm going to cross the Atlantic one day.
So, I must practice my swimming,
*   despite what you say.*
I know I can do it. I know that I can.
If you listen to me then you'll soon understand."
"I've listened," said Mother, "But what about you?
I called you and worried and what did you do?
You ignored me and swam in the lake night and day.
You're all wrinkled up, now what do you say?"

Allie looked at her mother, then she looked at the floor.
"I'm sorry," she said, *"we've been through this before.*
I really love swimming, can't you understand?
Have you ever done anything you thought was so grand?"
"I guess I'm beginning to see how you feel.
Now go and dry off and I'll cook a warm meal."
"Mom, what if I practice just during the day?
No nights, and no weekends. If that sounds okay. . ."
"Okay, I'll go with you, I'll give it a whirl.
I used to love swimming when I was a girl."

From that day on, they went swimming together,
Though Allison's mom didn't go in bad weather.
She helped Allison practice, she helped her be strong.
She even once let her swim all the night long,
As she watched with her flashlight, safe on the shore.
She had never seen such a great swimmer before.
She helped Allison train , even built her a pool.
Every day she helped Allison train after school.
And many years later, though her mother was frantic,
Allie followed her dream and she swam the Atlantic!

Snow

It's been a long time
since we had a big snowstorm,
something that everyone would call a blizzard,
and remember for ten years.
Snow deep enough for my sister to fall through,
so we could only see her hat.
Snow that we could build a snowman,
woman, and baby,
and also a pet dinosaur.
Snow that we could stay home from school for,
and pour orange juice on (to make slush.)
Snow so that my family had to walk
(instead of driving) to the market,
like a brave wilderness family,
having an adventure.
Cold, cold snow that would make your feet steam
if you took your boots off outside.

Johnny's Vacation

Johnny went on a vacation last June
to a beautiful beach with a turquoise lagoon.
His parents just loved it, they wanted to stay.
"Right out of the movies," his mother would say.

But in Johnny's opinion, the place wasn't dandy.
The sun was too hot and the sand was too sandy.
he begged of his parents, *"Please let me be,
I'll stay in our room and watch cable TV"*
"Stop whining!" Dad said, "play tennis, have fun."
"Come on, " said his mom, "go and play in the sun."

*"The ocean's too salty , I don't like to swim.
And when I build sandcastles , they always cave in."*
"But this beach, " said his mom, "is a dream come true.
The sand is so white and the water's so blue.
When you aren't playing tennis, you're catching a fish.
What more could a boy of your age ever wish?"

*"I like to wear sweaters. I like ice , I like snow.
I like to wear mittens wherever I go."*
"What?" asked his dad, "No tropical huts?
Are you crazy, my boy, are you totally nuts?"
*"I wish next vacation we'd go someplace cold.
Someplace way up north. It's great, I've been told.
I'll leave the hotel room and won't ever complain.
I'll even behave when we're taking the plane."*

"Well maybe," said Dad, "we can go just one time."
"Well maybe," said Mom, "though I like the beach fine.
Maybe next year we'll let Johnny have his choice.
He knows what he likes, so we'll give him a voice."
And then Johnny stopped whining,
and made this proclamation:
"We're all going to Alaska for next year's vacation!"

GRIMES
FAIRY
TALES
SAF

Messy Melissa

Messy Melissa, or so she was called,
was the messiest girl in the town.
She spilled milk, and left fingerprints on every wall,
she left toys, books, and clothes on the ground.

"Clean your room, please!" Melissa's mother would beg,
"Brush your hair and your teeth, wash your face."
"Melissa, this isn't a pig sty," Dad said
"this is a respectable place."

So Melissa would clean for a day, maybe two,
she'd fold all her clothes in her drawers.
She'd sweep and do laundry, she'd shampoo her hair,
(once she polished the knobs on the doors.)

But sooner or later she'd go back to her ways,
she'd leave buttery toast on the bed,
or she'd draw on the walls and have mud on her shoes,
(once she painted the puppy's ears red.)

One day Melissa came home from school
and was totally covered in hay.
"We went on a fieldtrip," she said to her mom,
"to a barn where some animals stay."

"Melissa!" Mom said, "There is hay on the rug,
not to mention your clothes and your hair.
Please clean yourself up,
you look like a mess,
and then vacuum it up over there."

"But Mom," said Melissa, "Why is there a rug?
I mean hay is so soft, and it's *free*..
If the horses and cows have hay on *their* floors
and it's fine for them, then why can't we?"

Melissa's mom got a *mom-look* on her face and
Melissa could tell she was thinking.
"I suppose if we didn't vacuum or sweep,
the housework would really start shrinking."

"Yahoo!" said Melissa, "Yahoo!" echoed Mom,
and they went to the farm to get hay.
At dinner that night when Dad came back home,
he didn't quite know what to say.

"Hay in our house? We have hay in our house?
Okay, let's try it and see."
Melissa sighed and so did her Mom,
so hay in their house it would be.

"Now that that's settled,
 Dad said with a grin,
"would somebody please pass the peas?"
Melissa went to reach for the peas,
but her elbow got stuck in her glass
and while she was trying to shake the glass off,
her food spilled on the floor with a crash.

There was milk on the floor and a hamburger, too,
the hay was all covered with cheese.
As Melissa tried to clean up this mess
she dropped the big bowl of peas.

The dog came bounding into the room,
ate the hamburger up in one bite.
Dad thought for a minute and then he announced
"I have a plan that might work, yes it might.

"We'll buy a cat to drink the milk,
find some mice to eat the cheese,
the dog has gobbled the hamburger,
but we need something else to finish the peas."

"I know, " said Mom, "We'll buy an ant farm.
The ants can eat whatever they please."

The very next night at dinner-time
when Melissa again spilled her food,
the animals happily ate it all up,
putting Mom and Dad in great moods.

But after dinner when Melissa's mom
went to her room to tuck her in,
she saw the clothes on the floor and the bed
and she instantly lost her grin.

"Melissa, please get those clothes off the floor,
we can't have good clothes in the hay!"
"But Mom, " Melissa argued with her,
"They'll just get dirty again anyway.

"Every time you wash your shirt,
you wear it then wash it again.
So really, it's all a big waste of time
just a cleaning cycle that never ends."

"You know, " said Mom, "You have a good point.
No more washing or ironing for me."
And with that she threw her sweater on the floor,
and sighed, "Ah, at last to be free."

"To be free of vacuuming, ironing, laundry,
to be free of sweeping the floor.
Thank you for showing me how not to care.
Do you mind if I put my gum on your door?"

When Melissa's dad came to tuck her in,
she noticed he smelled really nice.
"Dad, if you don't mind," Melissa said,
"I'll give you a little advice.

"You wake up so early five days a week
to get yourself ready for work.
You shower, you shave, brush your teeth, comb your hair,
you even put on a clean shirt.

"What if you wore your pajamas to work,
didn't shave, but just rolled out of bed?
You could sleep one more hour, relax, take your time,
and wear comfortable clothes, instead."

So the very next morning, Dad took her advice:
His hair was hanging over his eyes.
He was wearing pajamas and slippers
(Now wouldn't his boss be surprised!)

In fact, his boss was so angry,
he was fired that very same day.
"We don't need a man who's too lazy to dress,
and you smell like you're living in hay!"

Melissa came home from school that day,
all muddy and sad as could be.
"The mice ate all of my homework,
and my teacher gave me a 'D'."

Mom was preparing Dad's favorite dessert,
a chocolate cake from France,
but when it was time to serve it to him,
the cake was all covered with ants.

The three ate their dinner in silence,
the animals gathered near.
Melissa didn't spill any food,
she was neat from her toe to her ear,

"Maybe," she said, "We'd better be neat."
She looked sheepishly down at the floor.
She pushed aside the hay at her feet,
and then started to speak once more.

"We'll keep the cat and keep the dog,
let the mice and the ants go free,
then we'll sweep up the hay and wash the floors
and be happy, like we used to be.

"Dad can even brush his hair,
 Mom can iron her dress.
I never thought I'd be saying this,
but I'm awfully sick of this mess.

I'll clean my room, I'll wash my hair,
I'll even brush my teeth.
Not having to live in this pig-sty
will sure be a big relief."

So they all cleaned up that very night
and the next day Dad got back his job.
Mom made a cake that didn't have ants,
and no one at school called Melissa a slob.

Melissa was no longer messy,
though she still liked to roll in the hay,
"I like being clean," Melissa declared,
I like it better this way."

The Haunted House

I live in a haunted house.
It looks like any other house
 except it has more dust,
less furniture,
no glass in the windows,
the floor really creeks,
there are spiderwebs everywhere.
But I like it like that because I am a ghost.

One day a lady came into my house.
Her name was Priscilla.
Priscilla was just like a ghost
except that she wasn't see-through,
was born only 27 years ago,
walked instead of floating,
and, oh yeah, she couldn't go through walls,

Now most ghosts would have been scared of a person,
but not me, I was calm and collected
because after all, the house was mine.
"Get out of myyyyyyyyy house!" said Priscilla.
"But I was here first," I said.
"Oh really?" said Priscilla, *"We'll see about that!"*

"Oh really?" I said, "I have a right to live here.
I'm a ghost and you're only a person.
I need a house to haunt. You see,
I used to haunt an igloo and before that
I haunted a tent, but I want a real house to haunt,
just like all the other ghosts.
So to make a long story short,
I'm staying and you are going."

"Well I have a right to live here.
I'm a person and you're only a ghost.
I need a house to live in. You see,
I used to live in an igloo and before that
I lived in a tent, but I want a real house to live in,
just like all the other people.
So to make a long story short,
I'm staying and you are going."

"You lived in an igloo, too?" I asked.
"I have never met anyone before who has."
"I didn't know that ghosts lived in tents." She said.
"You know why we both like this house?"
I asked Priscilla. "it's because
we have so much in common."

"But you're a ghost and I'm a person."
She said to me, *"Don't you see?*
We just don't get along."
"Nonsense!" I said, "I bet we'd be great friends."
"I'm only friends with other people." she said.
"Well that's too bad" I said,
"because maybe if we got to know each other
we might even get along.
But if you really feel that way,
I'll just pack myself a peanut butter
and cucumber sandwich
and leave you alone."

Priscilla's eyes lit up. *"Did you just say
peanut butter and cucumber sandwiches?
They're my favorite."*
"They're my favorite too," I said.
"I'll make one for you if you want."
"You know," said Priscilla, *"I've never been friends
with a ghost before but you seem pretty nice."*

"Well," I said, "I've never been friends
 with a person before, but you don't seem so bad."
"Please don't move out." said Priscilla.
"I might get lonely and we have so much in common."

"Yes we do." I said.
 "I'd be happy to share the house with you."
"Great!" said Priscilla *"We'll be roommates."*
Then she walked into the kitchen to make a sandwich
and I floated through the wall.
Priscilla and I are different...
 and that's just as good as being the same.

The Special Guinea Pig

What's so special about a guinea pig, you ask?
Well for one thing, you could name him Lemmy
like I did.
You could also teach your guinea pig to do tricks
like riding a bicycle or tap-dancing.
And if those didn't work
you could teach him how to eat little food pellets.

What's so special about a guinea pig you ask?
Why a guinea pig could run for president or
be a famous actor or even a superhero.
However, if your guinea pig is anything like Lemmy
he might just choose to hang around in his cage
and sometimes he might escape from his cage
and hide behind the radiator
until my mother pokes him
with the end of the broom handle
and Lemmy runs out
and I feed him a food pellet
and I hug him and kiss him and tell him,
"Don't run away Lemmy... you're my best friend."

Now do you see why guinea pigs are so special?

What Do You Look Like?

If you were a tree,
what kind of tree would it be?
A tall dark pine? A coconut palm?
An oak tree with acorns?
What would it be?

If you were an animal,
would you be a shark?
A dog, perhaps? A spider?
A squirrel? a lark?

If you were a color,
would you be green or blue?
Red or mustard yellow?
or a mixture of the two?

These are good questions.
You can probably think of more.
And ask your friends to answer them.
You'll learn more about them, for sure.

A Girl Named Spike

Do you know Spike?
She likes ice cream and dogs.
She has a collection of gigantic frogs.
In the winter Spike likes
to build things out of snow
like snow-men and snow-women
and snow-hippos.

Spike likes to cook.
She likes making things up.
Once she even mixed mustard
with cake and ketchup.
She put it all in the blender
and put it on blend
it didn't taste great,
but Spike likes to pretend.

Spike once made up a song
then she made up a dance.
It involved spinning around
while you're holding your pants.
Spike sang her song
and recorded it five times
to listen to herself sing
without having to rewind.

Spike goes exploring
in her own backyard.
She's discovered ten species
of insects so far.
She found a car with no engine,
so Spike's building one.
"By the time I'm sixteen,
this baby should run!"

You don't know Spike?
That's her down the street
She's under that oak tree.
You guys ought to meet!

Spike's always lively,
she does her own thing,
but her spunk is part of
the joy that she brings.

About the Author

This is Hilary Weisman's first book of poetry.
She started writing poetry and stories when
she was about 8 years old.

Her plays for young audiences have delighted
school children for years. Her plays,*The First
Voyage of Christopher Columbus, The Salem
Witch Hunt,* and *A Land of Many Nations* , are all
published by Discovery Enterprises, Ltd.

When she's not recalling her youth through her
poetry, she's writing and directing films and
teaching filmmaking in Cambridge, Mass. In all of
her creative endeavors, her sparkling sense of
humor and her keen observations of people shine
through.

About the Illustrators

David H. Huckins illustrated his first book
for Discovery Enterprises, Ltd. in 1991, _W.E.B
DuBois: Crusader for Peace._ His whimsical illustrations on the cover, for _Johnny's Vacation_, _Snow_,
and for _When I Grow Up_ spring from his active
imagination.

Sheila Foley is both an illustrator and a writer.
She illustrated _Leonard Bernstein: America's Maestro_
and was the editor of _Faith Unfurled: The Pilgrim's
Quest for Freedom_ for Discovery Enterprises, Ltd.
In this volume of poetry, Sheila created the artwork
seen in _Messy Melissa_ and _The Swimmer,_